ZOOM!

Simon Armitage was born in 1963 in Huddersfield and grew up in West Yorkshire. After taking a degree in Geography at Portsmouth Polytechnic, he worked with young offenders for two years, and then went to Manchester University, where he gained a CQSW (Certificate of Qualification in Social Work), and as part of his MA wrote a dissertation on the psychology of television violence. He is now working as a probation officer in Oldham, and lives in Marsden, near, Huddersfield.

He won an Eric Gregory Award in 1988, and has published three pamphlets: *Human Geography* (Smith/Doorstop, 1986), *The Distance Between Stars* (The Wide Skirt, 1987), and *The Walking Horses* (Slow Dancer Press, 1988). In 1989 his work was featured in Radio 3's *New Voices* series.

His first book-length collection of poems, *Zoom!* (Bloodaxe Books, 1989), is a Poetry Book Society Choice.

SIMON ARMITAGE

ZOOM!

BLOODAXE BOOKS

ISBN: 1 85224 078 4

First published 1989 by
Bloodaxe Books Ltd,
P.O. Box 1SN,
Newcastle upon Tyne NE99 1SN.

Bloodaxe Books Ltd acknowledges
the financial assistance of Northern Arts

Typesetting by Bryan Williamson, Darwen, Lancashire.

Printed in Great Britain by
Bell & Bain Limited, Glasgow, Scotland.

Acknowledgements

Acknowledgements are due to the editors of the following publications in which some of these poems first appeared: *The Echo Room, Giant Steps, Harry's Hand, Iron, joe soap's canoe, Literary Horizons, London Magazine, The North, Orbis, Poetry Book Society Anthology 1989-90* (PBS/Hutchinson, 1989), *Poetry Nottingham, Poetry with an Edge* (Bloodaxe Books, 1988), *The Rialto, Slow Dancer, Smoke, Times Literary Supplement, Verse,* and *The Wide Skirt.*

Some of these poems were broadcast on *New Voices* (BBC Radio 3), and some were included in a collection for which Simon Armitage received an Eric Gregory Award in 1988. Many of these poems were previously published in three pamphlets: *Human Geography* (Smith/Doorstop Press, 1986), *The Distance Between Stars* (Wide Skirt Press, 1987), and *The Walking Horses* (Slow Dancer Press).

Cover photograph: Vaughan Fleming / David Parker / Science Photo Library.

Contents

Snow Joke

Heard the one about the guy from Heaton Mersey?
Wife at home, lover in Hyde, mistress
in Newton-le-Willows and two pretty girls
in the top grade at Werneth prep. Well,

he was late and he had a good car so he snubbed
the police warning-light and tried to finesse
the last six miles of moorland blizzard,
and the story goes he was stuck within minutes.

So he sat there thinking about life and things;
what the dog does when it catches its tail
and about the snake that ate itself to death.
And he watched the windscreen filling up

with snow, and it felt good, and the whisky
from his hip-flask was warm and smooth.
And of course, there isn't a punchline
but the ending goes something like this.

They found him slumped against the steering wheel
with VOLVO printed backwards in his frozen brow.
And they fought in the pub over hot toddies
as to who was to take the most credit.

Him who took the aerial to be a hawthorn twig?
Him who figured out the contour of his car?
Or him who said he heard the horn, moaning
softly like an alarm clock under an eiderdown?

On Miles Platting Station

the stitchwort has done well for itself, clinging
as it must to the most difficult corners
of near-derelict buildings. In the breeze
a broken cable mediates between the stanchions
and below the bridge a lorry has jack-knifed

attempting to articulate an impossible junction. This,
after all, is only a beginning. After the long
chicanery of the express train picking its way
across the fishplates we will rattle backwards
through the satellite towns. From Greenfield we will

fail to hold our breath the length of the tunnel
then chase the sixpence of the entrance and burst
the surface of light just over the border.
It will be the hour after rain. The streets will shine
and the trees bend, letting their soft load.

Until then, the platform holds us out against the townscape
high enough to see how Ancoats meshes with Beswick,
how Gorton gives onto Hattersley and Hyde, to where
Saddleworth declines the angle of the moor.
Somewhere beyond that the water in Shiny Brook

spills like a broken necklace into our village.
The police are there again; boxhauling the traffic,
adjusting the arc-lights. They have new evidence tonight
and they lift it from behind the windbreak, cradle it
along their human chain and lower it carefully down

into Manchester.

All We Can Do

The engine has less bite
than a baby's cough
so you nurse it into
the all-night forecourt.
David will come,
the cordage
of his half converted skip truck
clanging from streets away,
his bush-baby eyes
picking us out
in the battered kiosk.
He cleans the dip-stick
under his armpit
and tells us the car
has more faults
than he could shake a stick at.
But the sub-frame is sound
so he flips
the oily half tennis ball
from the knob of the tow-bracket
and couples us up
for the pull back to Huddersfield.
You sit with him
in the glass-backed cab, captive
to his fabulous tales
of strippers
at the Top Cat Club
and bearings that sheared
to the width of a tissue.
I steer and brake
in the car behind,
misreading the tangents
of the pavements and corners
as the gold
of each streetlight
burns
through your hairstyle.

Why Write of the Sun

when all it has done for us this last year
is dawdle in rain water smeared on the windscreen
or glisten carelessly across drying flagstones.
Take the week of the cottage in Anglesey:
just one afternoon to speak of when we flopped

like synchronised seals into Red Wharf Bay.
Then the drizzle came, the swingball splattered
like a dishcloth and a bike ride to Moelfre
blackened our spines with a plume of dirt.
After three sticky nights we called it a day.

Take the camping weekend under Malham Cove:
drunk with the effort of filling the air-beds
we saw stars spangle in the one-man tent.
Then we slept with a thunderstorm drum-rolling
over us, and dreamt of everlasting happiness

as we drifted apart on the waterlogged groundsheet.
Take the walk along the Humber Bridge
with the wind nagging the high-tension cables.
All we had to time the distance to the waves
was a spent match, and you told me to drop it.

Admittedly, there was one evening; mackerel sky,
the laburnum apparently cascading with yellow
and a breath of air almost saying something
through the trellis. But why write of whispering
when all we ever did that year was shout.

Greenhouse

It's gone to seed now; each loose pane pitted
with lichen like the walls of a fish tank,
the soffits lagged with a fur of cobwebs.
I burst in the other day; kicked the door
out of its warped frame, stood in the green light
among nine years of unnatural growth
and thought back to the morning we built it.
We used the old sash windows from the house,
held them flat with leather gloves, steadied them
down the path. I remember that journey:
you out in front, unsure of your footing
on the damp stones, and me behind counting
each of your steps through our cargo of glass.

Some nights I'd watch from my bedroom window
as you arrived home late from a concert,
and leaving the headlights on to guide you
waded into the black of the garden.
I'd wait, straining for the sound of the hasp
or guessing your distance by the sparkle
of a cufflink. When you disturbed them
the seeds of rose-bay willow-herbs lifted
like air bubbles into the beam of light.
Then you'd emerge, a hoard of tomatoes
swelling the lap of your luminous shirt;
and caught in the blur of double glazing
your perfect ghost, just one step behind you.

Night Shift

Once again I have missed you by moments;
steam hugs the rim of the just-boiled kettle,

water in the pipes finds its own level.
In another room there are other signs

of someone having left: dust, unsettled
by the sweep of the curtains; the clockwork

contractions of the paraffin heater.
For weeks now we have come and gone, woken

in acres of empty bedding, written
lipstick love-notes on the bathroom mirror

and in this space we have worked and paid for
we have found ourselves, but lost each other.

Upstairs, at least, there is understanding
in things more telling than lipstick kisses:

the air, still hung with spores of your hairspray;
body-heat stowed in the crumpled duvet.

Newton's Third Law

By the second year they were worlds away,
teasing knots from each other's hair at break
instead of baiting the school's mascot pig
or hauling first years through the long-jump pit.

They were peas in a pod; two blue-eyed blondes
who cocked a snook at Phyllis and Simone
as they were unaffectionately dubbed,
and held hands on the furthest playing fields

till the third year came and they shed their shells.
Once, two fifth years, having heard what they were
had them brace the back of a human chain
that was poised to touch the electric fence.

They jumped like salmon in a landing-net
but must have kept the taste. Geordie Jobson,
Head of Physics, burst a lung the day he
caught them through the prep room keyhole, testing

their charge on the gold-leaf meter after
kissing the Van de Graaff generator.

All Beer and Skittles

Strictly speaking, the facts are dimmer
than a NAAFI candle
and the details have clouded
like a plasterer's bucket.
But as the story goes
I try to stick by it.

He had a hair up his arse
at the best of times
and only stuck me on the payroll
as a long-forgotten family favour. Weekends were the worst
when he knew I had a match to play
but kept me behind on some half-baked errand

like painting the fall-pipes
or mixing the lampblack.
(The theory was he was chewing the cud
for his own son, Gideon, who was highly rated
but failed goalie trials
with Town and Preston.)

Anyhow, he was gone that weekend;
off 'on business' with a milliner from Spalding
leaving a list of jobs as long as his arm
and a warning against making
a poor fist of it.
As a footnote, he'd added

'Any problems – see Gideon.'
I was the early bird that morning,
collecting the van as the only named driver,
loading the blow-lamps, the fustian and tallow
then off to the café to pick up Fairbrother
who was not a full shilling

but a damn good worker.
After a bacon sandwich and a squint at the paper
we were rounding the corners
to Eastwood House
to lag the main tank and plumb in a toilet.
Gideon, we'd heard, would be along later.

He graced us with his presence
at ten past eleven and after half an hour
of picking and piking
he was sodding this for a game of soldiers
and angling for a lift into town
to buy fixing solution

and some bits for his camera.
Outside the shop I left the engine running
but true to form he was undecided
so I slung my hook and went for a coffee.
When I returned at twenty past three
he was still mulling over the coloured filters.

By the time we got back it was dropping dark;
Fairbrother had scarpered and Gideon's fizzog
said he couldn't be bothered.
This job, he assured me,
was a piece of piss and we'd sew it up tomorrow
by noon at the latest.

As his parting shot he tried to toe-poke
an iron ballcock
into the toilet
and his mouth fell open like an oven door
as it bounded on the rim
and the porcelain shattered.

The rest is history. The old man's weekend
was red sails in the sunset so he'd driven home early
to check on our progress.
At Eastwood House he found the overflow dripping
like a barmaid's apron
and the putty as dry as a Wesleyan wedding.

As he lifted the dust-cover
from the Twinflush De Luxe
it crumbled, then collapsed
like a hollow Stilton.
Gideon passed the buck;
I got my notice.

He knew his son was all mouth and trousers
but fair is fair, and family is family.
In any case, I fitted the bill,
me being the type who'd still suck his thumb
if dropped head first
in a barrel of bosoms.

What, with all this business,
a girl in the village getting herself pregnant
and Hutton retiring
at the end of the season,
I chose to ignore
the Deferment Papers

and was pulled for a stint
of National Service.
The boys in the barracks
have their own reasons: the unrequited love
of the postman's daughter
or their last five guineas

at Ripon Races.
And I like to think I've learned my lessons:
about eating shit
and the pecking order,
and the thickness of blood
and the thickness of water.

Don't Sing
(for Paddy McAloon)

The first time, we were saying grace when
the bump came right up through the table legs
and jumped a custard-apple out of the fruit bowl.
Maria excused us and even the dogs came running
to the garden to see what had happened.
It was a man. His arms and legs were splayed
into impossible positions and his head was bleeding,
gently, like a cracked egg, darkening the ground
to a rich brown. Isabel, bless her, said he looked
as though he were digging for worms, and the dint
was so deep we didn't need to dig a hole, just scrape
the topsoil across to bury him. We were popular
down in the village for weeks after.

The second time wasn't really ours because Giraldo
from the upper slope came down to ask us if
we might look in his pig-hut. He hoped it was
a star and wanted us to share in the good luck.
The roof was completely collapsed. He must have landed
straight across the dividing wall and exploded.
The pigs were already more than interested
and I had to forbid all five of the children
from looking. Any kind of burial was impossible
so we agreed that the next time a priest was around
he might say a few words inside the hut, and that
no one would go singing to the soldiers.

Giraldo knew of other stories from further north
where men had burst like melons onto the Chaco
or disappeared without a bubble in the soft sponge
by the river. And it isn't that we don't understand;
we do. It's how to tell the children something else.
Maria told the youngest that the men were plucked
by strong winds while sailing to Europe and one day
we might see boats fall out of the sky too.
But I'm worried about Jose. He's sixteen now
and knows a fairy story when he hears one.
What do I tell him the next time he asks
about the army helicopters heading for the clouds?
Or why the man in the potato-patch was stone cold?

It Ain't What You Do It's What It Does to You

I have not bummed across America
with only a dollar to spare, one pair
of busted Levi's and a bowie knife.
I have lived with thieves in Manchester.

I have not padded through the Taj Mahal,
barefoot, listening to the space between
each footfall picking up and putting down
its print against the marble floor. But I

skimmed flat stones across Black Moss on a day
so still I could hear each set of ripples
as they crossed. I felt each stones' inertia
spend itself against the water; then sink.

I have not toyed with a parachute chord
while perched on the lip of a light-aircraft;
but I held the wobbly head of a boy
at the day centre, and stroked his fat hands.

And I guess that the tightness in the throat
and the tiny cascading sensation
somewhere inside us are both part of that
sense of something else. That feeling, I mean.

The Bears in Yosemite Park

are busy in the trash cans, grubbing for toothpaste
but the weather on Mam Tor has buckled the road
into Castleton. A crocodile of hikers spills out
into a distant car park as the rain permeates

our innermost teeshirts, and quickly we realise:
this moment is one which will separate some part
of our lives from another. We will always remember
the mobile of seagulls treading water over Edale.

Killer whales pair for life;

they are calling across the base of the ocean
as we sprint for the shelter of the Blue John Mines.
We know the routine. In the most distant cavern
the lights go out and the guide will remind us

that this is true darkness and these splashes
of orange and bristling purple fibre are nothing
but the echoes of light still staining our eyelids.
Back in the car we peel off our sticky layers

and the stacks of rain

are still collapsing sideways as we gear down into
Little Hayfield Please Drive Carefully. On the radio
somebody explains. The bears in Yosemite Park
are swaggering home, legged up with fishing-line

and polythene and above the grind of his skidoo
a ranger curses the politics of skinny-dipping.
This is life. Killer whales are nursing their dead
into quiet waters and we are driving home

in boxer-shorts and bare feet.

Bus Talk

Of all the bloody cheek. How the hell would they feel
if they pulled their bathroom curtains back and found
the bottom of their garden slumped in the river
and their new greenhouse leaning over like a tent

with half the pegs pulled out? 'Don't worry Mr Argot,'
they said, 'your house is built on a plane of bedrock.'
Apparently it's the frost that's done this that and the other
to the soil. I said that might be very true

but the frost isn't going to put it back is it?
And the insurance won't pay. Sent a bloke round
with a spirit-level; couldn't have been here ten minutes
before he was up and off. I said listen, mate,

I used to be an engineer, I know subsidence
when I see it. He said it would have to look
like the Brighton bombing before they'd even think
of forking out. Don't you worry, pal, I said,

if you have to pull me out of the rubble
with my tackle hanging out and half the world there watching
I'll drag you through court so fast you won't know
if you're coming or going. I mean,

I don't know why he bothered coming round:
he didn't know goose shit from tapioca.
Only this morning the alarm clock had walked
to the edge of the drawers. It would have smashed

to smithereens but it went off and I woke up
and caught it. And I can't put eggs down anywhere.
No, if that house hasn't dropped a good two inches
this last eighteen months, my cock's a kipper.

Man on the Line

He didn't see me but his dog did:
tethered to the bridge, tugging at the rope lead
every now and again but going nowhere.
The railway draws a strange crowd before morning.

There's creeps like me spray-painting the carriages,
two nightwatchmen cursing this and that
from across the sidings; and him. He had
the map of Ireland written on his face.

I legged it before the cops came.
And they would come: diddy-jackets glowing like
street lamps, shovels sparking in the limestone chips.
This morning's milk train will be late into Leeds.

Phenomenology

Harold Garfinkel can go fuck himself.
This is a ten pound note. These are the keys
to your mother's car, and my father's suit
is nicely one half-size too big for me.

The tyres burst the puddles and the lamplight
spills like a moment from the past: only
to settle backwards, become distant and
still further distant in the long darkness

behind. Always we are moving away.
In the tunnel we test the echo of
the engine and check our haircuts in the
rain spattered quarter-light. Someday, something

will give. When the sun comes up tomorrow
it will dawn on us. But for now we shine
like the stars we understand: I think I'm
Tom Courtenay; you think I'm Billy Liar.

Don't Blink

Because the six year old on the pavilion steps
keeps stepping out of her mother's sling-back sandals
and a jogger on the road has barely enough breath
to say 'It never gets any easier, just quicker'
to his brother who is hoisting a double baby-buggy

over the narrow gate. Other things we can take
or leave: the ambulance that stubs its shock absorbers
on the sleeping policeman; the incensed batsman walking
back towards the bowler, saying if he does that again
he'll ram this steel-sprung Duncan Fearnley down his throat

or through the windscreen of his Ford Fiesta.
Not that this match could be close or anything;
the home team only have nine men and one of those
is the scorer's friend, who at a sensitive age looks
ridiculous in blue shorts and his sister's jumper.

Don't blink. You might miss the perfect smile
of a boy whistling 'Summer Time' who has to stop
when he gets to the bit that goes 'Your daddy's rich'
or the man with a dog who turns to ask his friend
why they can't make aeroplanes out of the same stuff

they make black-box flight recorders out of.
You might not even notice that an evening breeze
which wafts the drone of a moorland rescue helicopter
across the field from a mile away, is the same breeze
that chafes the tip from a pile of sawdust

and rocks the jumper of the left arm spinner, mislaid
for the moment, on the handle of the heavy roller.
The fight in the beer tent hardly gets a mention.
When the light fades, the swifts say more about the weather
than a poet ever could; picking up the smallest insects

dangerously close to the ground.

Dormobile

In the lay-by, for instance,
under the Kielder Dam
with the oil lamp
playing our huge shadows
on the red and white
striped concertina awning.

Or coasting up the drive
with the clutch dipped, its speed
wasting on the gentle slope; then
at the corner, the atlas
sliding back across the dashboard
to the driver's side.

Or in the garage;
the recoil of the seatbelts
ticking in and out of time against
metal cooling in the engine.
And the sidelights picking out
the shape of craneflies
whitewashed to the outhouse wall.

Or us, eating
in its tight kitchenette,
legs interlocked beneath
the fold-away table.
Then later in the drop-down bed,
shrinking from the zip, icy
down one side of the sleeping-bag.

And then on the coal road
when a cinder shot up
from under a snowplough
filling the windscreen
with something like cut diamonds.
You pushed a hole through the crazing;
brought us under control.

Can you see it, parked
where the hang-gliders push off from,
snug against the skyline?
Can you remember its shape,
not knowing from a distance
which way it was facing?

And You Know What Thought Did

If you could eat frost, you might think
it would crunch like an apple. You might think

that it forms in fruit like a snowflake forms
in the air. Crisp, and clear. Not so.

Frost in the flesh of an apple runs soft
and brown, and in California they smoke it out

with stove-like affairs that burn wood,
oil, paraffin or coal. Strange then, that

Californian apples are so sweet; so fresh;
because if you could eat smoke you might think

it would taste like a kipper. Not frost.

Getting at Stars
(from *The New Book of Knowledge:* QUA-STU)

The distance between stars is a calculation
of angles, orbits, lines of sight and partial perigons.
The size of a star is a function of its colour.

Stars do not twinkle; they are huge balls of fire
that would overwhelm us were they any nearer.
Thank heavens they are so far away.

The rays of light from the furthest stars
set off before the last grunt of the dinosaurs
but are bright enough to guide the flight of starlings.

Don't suppose for a moment that the stars are fixed;
each cluster is careering forward like a bolas. Even so, it's
safe for captains to steer their courses by them.

If Sirius were bound in this direction
at six times the speed of the fastest projectile
that ever left the muzzle of a great gun,

it wouldn't much trouble your great great-granddaughter
or even offset the next ice age. That crater
near Winslow, Arizona, is altogether another matter.

One cubic inch of a star in Ursa Minor
weighs well over a ton, and serves as a reminder
of the dangers of catching falling stars.

Those who travel to the stars and back will find
an added distance in their brothers' eyes.
The speed of light is a treacherous thing.

This Time Last Year

From a mile away, the superfine call
of a small girl barely carries itself
to the lawn where we sit. We picture her,
skipping perhaps or swinging a frayed rope
between herself and a fence post till it
wraps around her brother's legs, and jerks her,
drawing out that tiny voice towards us.
Dusk coming on now, slowly, and the roads
and walls give up their heat, just as the pearls
of condensation under the cold-frame
were eased away by the warmth of morning.
Strange, this detail at the two ends of day;
the starting up and slowing down of things.
Nothing now but to go inside; to leave
the wine bottles planted in the grow-bag,
ignore the football and the broken glass
and forget the cross-cut nap of the lawn,
smudged beyond interpretation. Nothing
but to shake the dead grass from the blankets,
to bundle the deckchairs into the house
and maybe pause in the doorway, watching.
We let the line of fire that ends itself
at the bottom wall of a burned out field
replace any red sky we had hoped for,
dying as it has done on other nights
against the last hill. And then we look up.
A thin stream of the cool air from outside
rocks the blind and chills the pillow cases.
We should have closed the windows; already
two moths are battering the bedside lamp,
drawn through the darkness from a mile away,
desperate to be where the only light is.

Very Simply Topping Up the Brake Fluid

Yes, love, that's why the warning light comes on. Don't
panic. Fetch some universal brake-fluid
and a five-eighths screwdriver from your toolkit
then prop the bonnet open. Go on, it won't

eat you. Now, without slicing through the fan-belt
try and slide the sharp end of the screwdriver
under the lid and push the spade connector
through its bed, go on, that's it. Now you're all right

to unscrew, no, clockwise, you see it's Russian
love, back to front, that's it. You see, it's empty.
Now, gently with your hand and I mean gently,
try and create a bit of space by pushing

the float-chamber sideways so there's room to pour,
gently does it, that's it. Try not to spill it, it's
corrosive: rusts, you know, and fill it till it's
level with the notch on the clutch reservoir.

Lovely. There's some Swarfega in the office
if you want a wash and some soft roll above
the cistern for, you know. Oh don't mind him, love,
he doesn't bite. Come here and sit down Prince. Prince!

Now, where's that bloody alternator? Managed?
Oh any time, love. I'll not charge you for that
because it's nothing of a job. If you want
us again we're in the book. Tell your husband.

Missed It by That Much

You had to borrow my sister's bike
and after a mile we stopped to lower the seat.
We chose that day because it was the first day
without rain for what seemed like a month.

We left our belongings hanging on the handlebars
and skirted the hedgerow for blackberries. Or was it
raspberries? I know my fingers were blue with the juice
and they stained the inside of the saddlebag.

There was smoke. They were burning stubble and the smoke
had bulged across the lane as we free-wheeled down
into the dip. You held your breath
and I think my chain came off.

This is what I remember the most: pushing the bikes
for over a mile, dropping like two cut flowers
then pointing out the landmarks down beneath us;
me stood, you leant against the trig-point.

The rest was all downhill.
I've been through since in the car and was surprised
by how much hadn't changed. I think you kept the map.
I was still learning to drive.

The Peruvian Anchovy Industry

The fat-bottom boats bob and roll
where the grain of the current planes the keel.
Sometimes they appear hand in hand; pair-trawling
where the surface is warm and the sea calm.

Sometimes they are almost stopped. The sonar arm
can pick the shoal up as an entity, then between the boats
the net falls open like a mouth and at its lips
the bright pelagic fish acquiesce.

Unless the cool 'El Nino' gusts westerly. That breaks
the light and then the catch becomes a poor resemblance
of a likeness of a shadow of itself. That sinks Peru
like in sixty-five, and seventy-one.

Today, two empty boats are drifting home across
the hollow fields of fished-out sea. The washed out crew
are puzzled by the ice-house; less than half full
and even the cormorants can't come up with anything.

Hard times for the hake and pilchard,
next on the U.S. shopping list.
Hard times for the Peruvian guano diggers,
no fish: no birds: no shit.

Poem

Frank O'Hara was open on the desk
but I went straight for the directory.
Nick was out, Joey was engaged, Jim was
just making coffee and why didn't I

come over. I had Astrud Gilberto
singing 'Bim Bom' on my Sony Walkman
and the sun was drying the damp slates on
the rooftops. I walked in without ringing

and he still wasn't dressed or shaved when we
topped up the coffee with his old man's scotch
(it was only half ten but what the hell)
and took the newspapers into the porch.

Talking Heads were on the radio. I
was just about to mention the football
when he said 'Look, will you help me clear her
wardrobe out?' I said 'Sure Jim, anything.'

B

Bylot Island

Arrived midday and it felt like heaven. Just the sun,
the sea, and the trace of jets across the sky.
Sorted out the test roster and Greg has worked wonders
with the lean-to. This is the real thing.

Sailed over to the old American DEW station today
and hung a college scarf on what's left of the mast. Noel
is an oddity. Hasn't spoken a word in two days.
He's a big bloke but I think I could handle him.

Took the first test this afternoon. Picked a catena
from the summit to the isthmus on the east side.
Even the yttrium samples are straight out of the text book.
Watched the dawn again. Wish we'd brought a football.

Greg has asthma. Bloody fool. Never mentioned it
to the faculty and now we're stuck with him.
Everyone is edgy. I spilt coffee in the variometer
which kind of evens everything up, I guess.

Hoar frost yesterday and the first snow this morning.
Both soil augers have snapped and I fought with Greg
over the food rations. I think we've patched it up
which is more than I can say for the inflatable.

More snow. Noel has cleared off with the one-man tent.
Saw him today on the plateau throwing snowballs
at the skuas and shouting at aeroplanes.
We must be under a flight path.

Didn't sleep at all last night. Greg was wheezing
like an old dog and the sleeping bags are sopping.
Woke up to find the drinking water had frozen.
Today is my birthday. Thought about Hilary.

Went outside this morning and saw Noel pissing
on the outboard motor. Is he nuts or what?
Anyway, tomorrow is the last day and I don't care
if he doesn't come back. Where the hell is he sleeping?

Had a cooked breakfast. Caught up with the reports
and Greg even swept out the lean-to. He's done well,
considering. As soon as the Vespucci docks I'll
explain the situation. Tell them about these two.

Rotten stinking bastards. Probably haven't left Resolute
with the zoologists yet. I'll kill Turner, the bastard.
Finished the last of the food and resigned ourselves
to another night of this. Still no sign of Noel.

Sat on the summit all day almost praying for the sight
of the ship coming into the skyline. Nothing.
What can I tell Greg. I'm watching him now walking
back up from the bay. I think he's been washing his hair.

Sometimes when the wind rattles through the awning
we imagine the traces of strong, familiar voices
calling our names. Our names. This is serious.
At night we listen for the sea freezing over.

Gone

Heaven, at last, to feel the thump
of the hearse door shutting out the light
and to settle between my brothers;
one at each side. We move off

gently, through the low gears as if
I was a serious patient; as if my blood
couldn't stand the slightest jolt of speed.
I suppose the rain, damping, or the specks

of rain on the face of my watch
will be everlasting. Of this day.
And I wanted to do so well. To
hold on to every difficult breath

and keep that release for the pain
of everyday things: the children; clothes;
a space where she might have spoken;
anything. Because it comes. And suddenly.

Maybe tonight. Not the bed, empty, that's
one thing. But her watch, still ticking
and the loop of one, blonde hair
caught in her hairbrush. That's another.

Girl

I had
no idea until
she backed into me

with a box
of oranges, turning
to apologise, letting

them drop. One
fell into my satchel
and we smiled.

I left it there;
not to eat,
just

happy
with the extra weight
and its smell

mixing into the books.
And I
passed by the stall

three times yesterday;
slowly, on
no particular errand.

Screenplay

The sun puts its colour on the curtains
and plays on the pink film of their eyelids;
so, even as they sleep, light is shaping
the closing moments of their different dreams.
He sees the girl in the paisley bandeau
picking her way down the awkward cliff path
and he follows her, careful of his step.
He plans their meeting. Does she have the time?
Is this hers, this comb he found in the rocks
and wasn't that the highest jet ever
scoring its course in silver above them?
Something bothers him, but nevertheless
he slips the simple knot of her headband
and lets the corn of her hair come spilling
from its neatly twisted stook. Already
he's guessing the colour of her toothbrush.

In her sleep she sets an easel facing
the heat haze and sees detail emerging
from the afternoon calina. Those lines
for instance, the zinc roofs of poor houses
or maybe the lips of vine terraces.
And those clumps of green; cypress trees perhaps
split by an unmetalled road or a path
that leads to a structure on the hilltop:
a tracking station or a monastery.
Her brush strokes mimic the uncertainty.
When the boy with the olive skin comes by
she asks about the never-ending dust,
and with sign language and broken English
tells him how it marks the cracks in her hands.
No couch grass striping her soft leather shoes
with cuckoo-spit here she thinks. No clover.

When they wake they dress in the loosest clothes,
skip breakfast and head for the tennis courts.
He explains that the sun shines every day
but cloud cover spoils the weather. She rates
these days as the kind in which you least mind

having to go sailing with your parents.
It's the closest they can come to saying
what it is to walk out into the world.
Too tired to even knock-up, they stroll on
and though they clip each dandelion clock
with the full face of their rackets, the seeds
just parachute slowly forwards, marking
the slightest effort as a waste of time.
When their hands brush they link fingers and smile;
each unaware of their separate nights,
each sensing the warmth of the other's skin.

Simon Says

Through the window of the train the houses shake
like out-takes from a hand-held cine-film
until the tube goes underground, and then the light
picks out a cable running close alongside.

Who is this guy at Seven Sisters who smells
like an attic; who wants to frighten me by
tugging at my cuffs, by shouting without words
and squeaking like a wet balloon? He is deaf

and dumb and I speak to him like a goldfish.
His eyes roll. He touches his pale, milky fingers
to my lips and tests the weight of each word, he
catches every word. We are sat on the floor

to play this game: he puts his hand against
his drawing pad and makes me trace again and again
with a crayon the outline of its simple shape.
We share a smile. I have to leave. He is frantic

but only for a second as he sets off
down the train, pictures of perfect hands slipping
from his folder, waving for a moment in the air
then landing by the shoes of other passengers.

Lamping

I can half hear you John, half see you fumble
with a car battery, a two-two air rifle,
two wires and a headlamp. You and that shivering dog
going as two silhouettes above Warrington.

These things too. The red spot of your cigarette
as the only touch of colour till the filament
snags its circle through the eyes of a rabbit.
Then the trigger as you pull it, then the pellet

punching a dark red pit in the rabbit's neck.
Then you whistling, pointing for the dog to collect
and drop it at your feet like a lame excuse.
And the red tail lights tucked between the van's legs.

Then this. Its four lucky feet and lucky white tail
dangling from a peg on the garage wall,
and the rest, dropped like off-cuts in the dustbin,
too small to eat and too big for a keyring.

Poem by the Boy Outside the Fire Station

Anyway, I'm mad. I know this as a fact
because him in the Post Office said I was.
He tried to tell Joey when he cashed his Giro
and he knows damn well I'm not deaf.

I just like watching. Have you seen how clean it is?
Clean as a kitchen. Cleaner. I had a good look
last week before they closed them concertina doors.
Cleaner than the bloody Post Office anyway.

And I like how they're always half dressed.
It's like a scrum in that cabin when they set off,
buttoning their flies up or getting into their boots right.
Anne says they argue about ringing the bell.

Dibber, he's only a part-time volunteer, says
he's only ever missed a call-out once
when he was getting to the pitch with his missis.
He reckons they'll get them bleeper things in next year.

I'm always ready, watching when the siren goes
and they pile out of their houses in pyjamas,
pulling them blue jerseys over their heads
and wobbling down Manchester Road on their bikes.

Him at the Post Office knows I'm up to something.
Well, I stink of petrol, and he's seen my matches
and he knows damn well I don't smoke.
But he's frightened to death of saying anything.

Dykes

Our fingers touched near Lelystad. We were poring over plans
of coastal reclamation in the Netherlands

and from there she took the upper hand. Later I discovered
she was only pointing to an overflow culvert.

Although we were close she knew a closer, deeper circle
which at seventeen I found undetectable

and many of her stories held no water
especially those involving Maureen, Jane or Wanda.

It took a friend in English Literature
to pity me and puncture my naivety

with what he knew 'instinctively'. He told me they were 'Dykes'
and took delight in passing on his viewpoint, how at night

they swapped their sickly sweet secretions
or plugged each other with their fingers,

and how they recognised a common truth
of 'only put in yourself what you'd put in your mouth.'

At school they checked each other's Geography,
lovingly, and spoke above our range of hearing,

while we, obviously seventeen and badly shaven
made lots of noise around the football table.

A Painted Bird for Thomas Szasz

It was his anorak that first attracted me.
The foam lining was hanging from a split seam
and a tear that ran the length of his back was patched
with sellotape and sticking plaster. So I watched
as he flitted between the front seats of the bus
and fingered the synthetic fur around his hood.

The next time I noticed was at the terminus
where he was pretending to direct the buses.
From then there was a catalogue of incidents,
moments and locations where we coincided,
and each time I watched him talking to the drivers
who ignored him, and jotting down the route numbers.

One particular time he was in the arcade
eyeing the intricacy of a timetable.
He caught me watching the reflection of his face
so he exhaled onto the surface of the glass
and wrote his name on it. Billy. I passed by him,
breathing in, and he smelt like a wet dog, drying.

Another time I noticed more than I meant to
was a lunchtime at the Probation Day Centre
where I squinted through the gap in the serving hatch
to see him watching the traffic on the bypass.
His focus settled on a simple bicycle
which he followed till it slipped below the skyline.

I also saw him, once, in the covered precinct
pissing himself through his pants onto the concrete
and fumbling with the zip on his anorak.
He bothered me, and later I had to walk back
across where the dark circle of his stain had grown
and was still growing, slowly, outward, like a town.

Heron

You pull onto the soft verge
and the tyres slacken into the dirt.

I pass the field-glasses
from the glove compartment
and you fumble, finding a focus
through the action of the wipers

and describe it to me: how it
hangs in the shallows, shaking the rain
from its featherings. How it watches,
then cautiously adopts

its fishing position, then wades
thoughtfully forward, then holds again.
You go on piecing out the picture
and I affect not to listen

until you put the glasses down
and I realise you've stopped talking.
We sit there, breathing, steaming up
the windows and watching

as the heron feints
to a fleck on the line of the lake
like a wood-chip flaw
on slate Ingres paper,

and the hilltops are water-marked
if we look hard enough.

Angoisse

The sun bled into the corner of his eye
but his sweat didn't. Every ten minutes he wiped
his forehead with the underside of his shirt sleeve
and settled back into the sand and his sleep.

If the flies bothered him he never showed it.
Three tankers passed the point and he hardly noticed.
He was vaguely aware of another figure
but the slant of the heat haze made him unsure.

Even asleep the colour of the sun weighed
like the tangent of an orange on his eyelids.
He watched it for an hour, and it flickered once
as a shadow passed quickly across his face.

At three o'clock he licked the salt from his lips
and stood up. He shook the sand from his shoes and socks
and looked for the leather case with his glasses in.
He was thirsty and his wallet was missing.

The best stones at the side of the road were blunt
and he ran the blade of his knife across his thumb.
What now, with the sun bursting from behind the head
of the other man swaggering down the road?

Back home he quartered an orange with the knife
and the juice on the blade pearled into droplets like
the first beads of a cold sweat. He took a towel
and wiped it. It was done. He had killed no one.

November

We walk to the ward from the badly parked car
with your grandma taking four short steps to our two.
We have brought her here to die and we know it.

You check her towel, soap and family trinkets,
pare her nails, parcel her in the rough blankets
and she sinks down into her incontinence.

It is time John. In their pasty bloodless smiles,
in their slack breasts, their stunned brains and their baldness,
and in us John: we are almost these monsters.

You're shattered. You give me the keys and I drive
through the twilight zone, past the famous station
to your house, to numb ourselves with alcohol.

Inside, we feel the terror of dusk begin.
Outside we watch the evening, failing again,
and we let it happen. We can say nothing.

Sometimes the sun spangles and we feel alive.
One thing we have to get, John, out of this life.

Still for Sale

The landing radiator must have been leaking. Its water
has stained five fingers down the wooden staircase
to where it evaporates one step from the bottom,
appearing to have run out of ideas.

Even the March sun looks changed as it splinters
off the chrome on the fold-away camp bed.
There are no curtains to soften its edges
and the pelmet is propped up by the bookcase.

You call out 'Simon' in an empty room downstairs
while directly above I bend to a bottom drawer
where you kept my first cautionary letters.
I know there will be nothing in it.

In the half-converted barn your father's box files
protrude like elbows from a bin-bag.
Some others are tossed in an orange crate
just as they were left by the Official Receiver.

The rainbow mobile cast into the corner
is a complication of ceramics and fishing line.
We used to count as it played its seven colours
on the ceiling, twisting near the open window.

I run my finger through the dust on a table
and comment on it, while you go on sniffing
at a suggestion of damp in the walk-in wardrobe.
The six tennis rackets in there still look good to me.

The old school atlas we came for has been thrown away
so we count the months the house has been empty
and close the door, firmly. I turn the car round
while you post the keys back through the letterbox.

Home on the Range

There are breadcrumbs, staples,
eyes of potatoes which you hide
at reference points
on the patterned carpet.

Mostly, I miss them.
There are gloves
in the sock-drawer, white ones
which you trace

around the inside
of the guitar and across
the chimney-breast.
I fail this test.

There are pills, one
for every morning
which you take each morning
on the way to work.

And there are words, some words
which we cannot speak:
Baby. Alicia.
Shotgun. Cathedral.

Advertisement

For a poem in which two characters
not dissimilar to ourselves walked hand in hand
through the backstreets of post-war Rome
and were cruelly misguided by its cast of non-actors.
It was Sunday, and every belfry insisted
on shaking out its table-cloth of doves. Later,
the rain which had threatened in a previous scene
could hold no longer and the men and women
on the steps of the Vittoriana
rose like the rigging of a bottled ship
before separating into different doorways.

But despite its apparently dated conventions
it was also a poem of social criticism
which examined the lot of the working man
with incisive simplicity and disarming vision.
Consequently it was of the type which is highly praised
but largely unprofitable and forced its creator
to seek temporary employment
as a rural police officer to finance his art
and his complicated family.
It was not the deeply human work of another poem,
perhaps its sequel, but nevertheless
it had tenderness and sincerity to spare
and boasted the development of an impasse situation:
of doors and windows that would not open,
of taxis that never arrived, or did arrive
but failed to stop, or stopped eventually
only to begin a nightmare journey
through mile after mile of familiar but unmapped territory.
The film version is a different story;
it is widely accepted as a supreme achievement
and a reminder that neorealism in its pure form
is more than an artistic style,
it is a way of life.

Eyewitness

As you will appreciate, these contact lenses
are not binoculars,
my acuity is not what it used to be
and the pollen count
was astronomical that day. But if I said
the rear view mirror
and the wing mirror and the windows
made a kaleidoscope
which turned his yellow teeth through each
of its facets
I could hardly be accused of distortion.
Please bear with me.
I will take for granted your understanding
that conjecture
is anathema to me, but even the layman
could not have failed
to notice something furtive in his gait;
something circumspect
about his manner. Clearly the embankment
was a vantage point
with which he had not reckoned. The knife
for instance,
a polished thing of the bowie type
was raised
at an angle on which I need not elaborate
and though the mist
was soupish and the level-crossing bumpy
would I be lying
if I said his upper lip trembled like the lip
of a man
on the brink of an incident? I would not.
Whatever happened
after that is anybody's business, but clearly
the dog was not restrained
and an ambulance would have struggled
in that traffic.
Am I making myself transparent?

Resonant Frequencies

He was cramming in a carrel at Central Library,
leafing his way through *Science in History*

for a quote to preface his latest thesis
on the impact of wind on suspension bridges.

Imagine, for example, a tuning-fork
stopped by the action of a stroboscope

then touched on the rim of a cut glass goblet;
the goblet would burst at the moment of contact.

There were other, more recognised lines of inquiry
but since his expulsion from the Royal Society

he had pulled the plug on printed circuits,
turned a blind eye to fibre optics,

ignored the attraction of electromagnets
and gone off at his own unorthodox tangent.

Returning to the text he circled a structure
which once spanned a great American river

but had buckled in the eye of some storm or other
and flipped its passengers into the water.

I pictured a man taking leave of his motor;
wobbling from the fast lane towards the hard shoulder.

An Ornithology of the Americas

On the morning after the house-warming party
we could do worse
than gather round the unlicensed portable
as an international team of assorted scientists
free-fall to a Venezuelan table-top mountain.
The biologist's compound fracture is shocking,
but even as we speak
the pollen spores from the surrounding lowlands
are dusting this elevated island,
carried skyward by the warm thermals
or in the leg-feathers of the deafening macaws.
Only the cicerone looks at home
as he guides a stream of drinking water
down an aqueduct of maize leaves;
and true to form, just as the speleologist
stumbles on a fossil of great significance
they are airlifted out in a helicopter gunship
under the aegis of this month's government.

It is difficult to know where to begin.
Should we wrest Caracas from the Spanish yoke
before breakfast, or empty the ashtrays
and make a start on the dishes?
The news is all El Salvador and Nicaragua
and the rain outside is irresistible
so we drive Ann to the station
and fall for the regularity of the wipers
as they sweep aside
everything the elements can throw at them.
Back at the house the mystery of the condor
whose image is etched in the oxidised crust
of the Nazca Plain is still a mystery despite
the beautifully illustrated *New Book of Knowledge*;
and in the afternoon
after the morning after the night before
we could do worse than agree,
in principle at least, that the eagle has landed.

Canard

We first crossed swords in The Duke of Marlborough
when his cue ball jumped from the threadbare table
and came like a comet
through the smog in the tap room
to break the ice
in my whisky and water.

I declined the offer of his polka dot neck tie
to soak the spirits
from my moleskin trousers,
but when he stumped up for a brandy and soda
we were well on the way
to burying the hatchet.

Poetry was rhubarb. Books were for eggheads.
The Sport of Kings was the only diversion
and before I had time
to say Jack Robinson
he had lifted a biro from my inside breast pocket
and indented a message on my Gauloises packet:

Calliope, two o'clock, Market Rasen.

My stomach was tighter than a baby's fist
as the s.p. crackled through the p.a. system
and my hands were flapping
like a cabbage white as I forked out a fiver
on the nose of that filly. It cakewalked
the field like a hot knife through butter,

and ten minutes later I was fifty pounds wiser.
He was propped in the snug of The Star and Garter
with a pint of Guinness
that was over-enthusing,
and after a chaser for medicinal purposes
he did me the honour of revealing his sources.

Later, in the men's room of The Coach and Horses
he revealed the extent
of his other intentions.
Our liaisons, he suggested, could be purely ironic,
like the coming together of two great rivers:
productive, creative, but not embryonic.

Somewhere Along the Line

You met me to apologise, you were saying
as we waited in the drizzle for the slow train.
When it focused in we said goodbye and we kissed
and from the window you were caught; teary and fixed.

You ran across the wooden bridge, I knew you would,
to get down on the other platform and to wave,
but as you did the eastbound Leeds train flickered past
and ran you like a movie through its window-frames.

I keep those animated moments of you as
our catalogue of chances rushed and chances missed.

Potassium

Finally, under the tree
with the heart-shaped leaves,
avoiding the clutches
of orange insect eggs

she lifted her head
through ninety degrees of light
and let the soft, red
bubble of her mouth break

gently into my own.
We were both thirteen.
From a washing-post
by the flaky outhouse door

her anxious sister was coming,
ready or not.
The box-room was south-facing
and through a bull's-eye

in the window
the concentrated light
had scorched a semicircle
into the lino. Later,

on the wharf
we would inch our way
round a washed-up cuttlefish,
poached and bleached

in its own purple tide-mark.
At breakfast, someone's camera
punched the air with silver
and the man

with no luggage was framed
in the serving-hatch. In the bay
a boat race
began with a firework.

From an unmarked ketch
the authorities watched him
feeding scraps of metal
from the car-deck to the seagulls,

which exploded. They
soaked up the pieces
with sand
from the fire-buckets

and led him away
as the dormobiles
were loading
and unloading.

Whatever she said
from the end of the jetty
was nothing
compared with the roar

of the engines. Through
the fog the mainland
was always
just beginning.

Social Inquiry Report

I interviewed him twice: once at his home,
once from the back seat of his shooting-brake
with his mangy dog on the soft-top roof,
its tail curling in through the quarter-light.

He'd bought the cars from a friend in Bolton
then sold them. He'd never done a wrong thing
in his life so imagine his surprise
when the law turned up and arrested him.

We sat and watched as the metal crusher
cubed a written-off Morris Traveller
and listened to the panel-beaters send
their muffled echoes into Manchester.

I lent weight to his side of the story
but they sent him down. In the holding-cell
he shook like a leaf but feigned a handshake
to palm me two things: a key to his house

to turn off the water, and a fiver
for dog food and a gallon of petrol.

Bempton

Things have come
to this pretty pass:
me hiding, half covered
with dead grass,

your voice rummaging –
a pig after truffles.
A breeze, the silver
underside of leaves

like a shoal of fish
that changes direction.
Pooh sticks
and a plastic clipper,

first to the weir.
What else?
Shadows beside themselves.
The time of year.

A Hillman Imp, a roof rack,
the beak
of an upturned canoe
overshooting its windscreen.

A bridge. A tree
gone septic where we gouged
our initials.
That old chestnut.

Eighties, Nineties

Firstly, we worked in laughable conditions.
The photocopier
defied definition,
the windows were sealed with a decade of paintwork,
the thought of a cigarette triggered the sprinklers
and the security door
was open to question.
Any excuse got me out of the office.

I found the letter in the 'pending' folder,
a handwritten thing
signed T. Ruth O'Reilly
on a perfumed leaf of watermarked vellum.
It requested recognition, or maintenance even
from a putative father,
one William Creamstick
who was keeping shtum in the Scottish Borders.

At midnight I took the decision to risk it.
I darned the elbows
of my corduroy jacket,
threw a few things in an old army surplus
and thumbed it to Ringway for a stand-by ticket.
At dawn I was still
going round in circles
in a five mile stack over Edinburgh airspace.

I accepted a lift to Princes Street Gardens
from an aftershave rep
who slipped me some samples.
It was Marie Celeste-ville in the shopping centre
so I borrowed a pinta from the library doorstep
and a packet of rusks
from the all-night chemist
then kipped for an hour in the cashpoint lobby.

Creamstick's house was just as I'd pictured:
pigs in the garden,
geese in the kitchen.

He was toasting his feet on the coal fired Aga
as I rapped the window with my umbrella handle
and he beckoned me in,
thinking I'd come
to spay the bitches in his sheep-dog's litter.

He listened, nodding, as though I were recounting
the agreeable facts
from another man's story.
Then producing a bread knife the size of a cutlass
he suggested, in short, that I vacate his premises
and keep my proboscis
out of his business
or he'd reacquaint me with this morning's breakfast.

In a private wood on the way to the trunk-road
I stumbled on a fish farm
and beyond its embankment
was a fish that had jumped too far from the water.
Two more minutes of this world would have killed it.
I carried it, drowned it,
backstroked its gills
till it came to its senses; disappeared downwards.

Back at Head Office they were all going apeshit.
Hadn't I heard of
timesheets, or clearance,
or codes of conduct, or agency agreements?
As I typed out my notice and handed my keys in
I left them with this
old tandem to ride on:
if you only pay peanuts, you're working with monkeys.

You Are Here

Thousands of miles have rattled beneath the tyres
since the evening when I almost told your father
to f**k off, and your mother will swear to God
that her pulse is slower and will offer us
her delicate wrist where the blood beats confidently.

Happily for everyone he has put down anchor
on the east side of the borough, but sometimes
your half-sister or half-brother will gesture
in a way too close for comfort, a likeness
remarked upon only in passing.

In any case you sleep now, held in suspension
by the arm of the seat belt, cradled in its sling
like a slowly mending fracture as I thread the car
through mile after mile of contra-flow or wake you
on the roundabouts the other side of Leeds.

Tomorrow, stood before the push-button town plan
we might work our way through the local attractions
or even visit them, bearing in mind
that everything is relative to the one, strong light
which, for now, describes our position perfectly.

The Civilians

We signed the lease and knew we were landed.
Our dream house: half farm, half mansion; gardens
announcing every approach, a greenhouse
                    with a southern aspect.
                    Here the sunlight lasted;
evenings stretched their sunburnt arms towards us,
held us in their palms: gilded us, warmed us.

We studied the view as if we owned it;
noted each change, nodded and condoned it.
We rode with the roof down, and if the days
                    overstepped themselves
                    then the golden evenings
spread like ointment through the open valleys,
buttered one side of our spotless washing.

Forget the dangers of iron pyrites
or the boy who ran from his mother's farm
to the golden house on the other hill
                    which was a pigsty
                    taking the sunlight.
This was God's glory. The big wheel had stopped
with our chair rocking sweetly at the summit.

For what we have, or had, we are grateful.
                    To say otherwise
                    would be bitterness
and we know better than to surrender.
Behind the hen-house the jalopy is snookered:
                    its bodywork sound,
                    its engine buggered
but still there is gold: headlights on the road,
the unchewable crusts of our own loaves,
                    old leaves the dog drags in.
                    Frost is early this autumn.
                    Wrapped up like onions
we shuffle out over the frozen ground;
prop up the line where our sheets are flagging.

Ten Pence Story

Out of the melting pot, into the mint;
next news I was loose change for a Leeds pimp,
burning a hole in his skin-tight pocket
till he tipped a busker by the precinct.

Not the most ceremonious release
for a fresh faced coin still cutting its teeth.
But that's my point: if you're poorly bartered
you're scuppered before you've even started.

My lowest ebb was a seven month spell
spent head down in a stagnant wishing well,
half eclipsed by an oxidized tuppence
which impressed me with its green circumference.

When they fished me out I made a few phone calls,
fed a few meters, hung round the pool halls.
I slotted in well, but all that vending
blunted my edges and did my head in.

Once, I came within an ace of the end
on the stern of a North Sea ferry, when
some half-cut, ham-fisted cockney tossed me
up into the air and almost dropped me

and every transaction flashed before me
like a time lapse autobiography.
Now, just the thought of travel by water
lifts the serrations around my border.

Some day I know I'll be bagged up and sent
to that knacker's yard for the over spent
to be broken, boiled, unmade and replaced,
for my metals to go their separate ways...

which is sad. All coins have dreams. Some castings
from my own batch, I recall, were hatching
an exchange scam on the foreign market
and some inside jobs on one arm bandits.

My own ambition? Well, that was simple:
to be flipped in Wembley's centre circle,
to twist, to turn, to hang like a planet,
to touch down on that emerald carpet.

Those with faith in the system say 'don't quit,
bide your time, if you're worth it, you'll make it.'
But I was robbed, I was badly tendered.
I could have scored. I could have contended.

Hunky Dory

It will not hurt
to wait, unetherised, in a high leather seat
and be tipped to the light.
And it will not hurt at all
to roll one sleeve past the crook of the elbow

and offer a long pale forearm.
The auxiliary nurse is an old retainer: a slow
methodical man in carpet slippers who delivers
a purple bauble of methylated spirits.
His free hand cups the flame.

He swabs from the wrist upwards, tattoos
a roll call of allergies with a gold biro, full stops
each word with a separate pipette
then runs through each drop
with a burnt needle. It is no problem.

Similarly, in radiography, it is no trouble
to be laughingly bundled up to the template,
to be minutely adjusted, and later, with the negatives
against a clear blue sky
what cannot speak cannot lie:

my stupid grin, my empty eyes,
my hollow head. Everything is O.K. Outside,
a warm front from Europe breezes in. No snow
this Christmas, no kristallnacht of ice
to shatter the puddles. The tattoos

I have left intact, a heat rash
still expands the word CAT, proof that the kittens
will have to go
or be banned from the bedroom
at the very least. I kick them out

but they sulk in the garden,
and when I relent they flounce in
like ruined children,
curl their noses at the top of the milk
and will not be loved.

The Visitor

This is
a hard one to explain away: your tall
long-standing Fräulein arriving
unannounced on my doorstep with a toothbrush
and the clothes she stands in. I bundle her inside;

so much laundry before the cloudburst
and for an hour at least she sits and teases
particular fibres from her coat lining, declines
all manner of refreshment.
But we have all night.

Two in the morning. Everywhere we telephone
you are elsewhere; out apparently
in thick rain walking the parish boundary,
circling the house
where your mother holds fort, or any house

where my guest's impeccable English might ring out
and deceive you. We imagine you emerge
like a man dipped in silver, one quarter of the moon
enough to colour and usher you out of the bottom field,
see you clear

of the nettles. Four or five more strides
will bring about the view
you have outlined so graphically: two roads parting,
their streetlights marking a flawless
almost unbelievable Y.

Tomorrow you fish
for the full story. You know my house,
enough blankets
to sleep the whole Rhine Army
but one bed only.

And we will not speak of taking sides.
Only that she left as arranged, likening
your mother's hatchback to a Black Maria.
Then our exchange; my 'Isn't that what friends are for?'
And your 'Some day

I'll do the same for you Buddy. Don't worry.'

The Stuff

We'd heard all the warnings; knew its nicknames.
It arrived in our town by word of mouth
and crackled like wildfire through the grapevine
of gab and gossip. It came from the south

>   so we shunned it, naturally;
>   sent it to Coventry

and wouldn't have touched it with a barge pole
if it hadn't been at the club one night.
Well, peer group pressure and all that twaddle
so we fussed around it like flies round shite

>   and watched,
>   and waited

till one kid risked it, stepped up and licked it
and came from every pore in his body.
That clinched it. It snowballed; whirlpooled. Listen,
no one was more surprised than me to be

>   cutting it, mixing it,
>   snorting and sniffing it

or bulking it up with scouring powder
or chalk, or snuff, or sodium chloride
and selling it under the flyover.
At first we were laughing. It was all right

>   to be drinking it, eating it,
>   living and breathing it

but things got seedy; people went missing.
One punter surfaced in the ship-canal
having shed a pair of concrete slippers.
Others were bundled in the back of vans

>   and were quizzed, thumped,
>   finished off and dumped

or vanished completely like Weldon Kees:
their cars left idle under the rail bridge
with its cryptic hoarding which stumped the police:
'Oldham – Home of the tubular bandage.'

Others were strangled.
Not that it stopped us.

Someone bubbled us. C.I.D. sussed us
and found some on us. It was cut and dried.
They dusted, booked us, cuffed us and pushed us
down to the station and read us our rights.

Possession and supplying:
we had it, we'd had it.

In Court I ambled up and took the oath
and spoke the addict's side of the story.
I said grapevine, barge pole, whirlpool, chloride,
concrete, bandage, station, story. Honest.

B & B

It's easier than falling off a log.
Down south they call it doing a runner
but for us it is an art form of course.
Swanning round the foothills of The Cobbler
we are model tourists in every way:
keeping to the paths, following the code,
upbraiding litterlouts at every turn.
And then the dead mole: soft as a pocket,
perfect like a small velvet purse whose snout
we might unclasp and silver down inside:
money enough for tonight's feast. The soup
at the side of the bowl is coolest.

Nothing as cheap as an open window
or shinning down a drainpipe at midnight
or down paying a suitcase full of bricks.
To our hosts we are almost cousinly
who pity my grasp of their mother tongue.
This morning I was the stupid Polack
fetching his O.S. map from the camper,
but as they sketched a foolproof route for Ayr
we were sashaying all the way to Largs
with a fortnight's free board under our belt
and two packed lunches for the trip. A smile,
after all, is two sneers on the same lip.

The Monday had been a proper scorcher.
After readjusting the numberplates
and lapping heather into the front grille
we set down in a passing-place and basked
in our finest hour. Promising fresh trout
for breakfast we had risen with the lark
and to this day she will swear us both drowned.
It was dark. The wall was down. Arm in arm
along the bank with slow dégagé steps
we had seen the cordon as a handrail;
shown ourselves into the river. The sun,
not the storm, will remove a man's blazer.

Team Lada

Like chalk and cheese our politics: mine read
from blackboards and the books you forked out for,
yours swallowed whole, handed down on a plate,
no red Leicester, all blue Stilton. That said,

those winter mornings found our Russian cars
nose to tail in true Politburo style,
and us half asleep, boxed in their cabins,
yawning like a pair of pre-packed orchids.

Evenings too found us bumper to bumper
racing home to burnt suppers; late, but with
a bouquet of excuses, keeping mum
about pit stops at the Coach and Horses.

Twice, while working alternate shifts we passed
in the cutting: me done, you just starting.
The first was a joke: I caught you smoking
that fat cigar against doctor's orders.

But the second…I wanted to warn you:
black ice, low cloud, a speed trap; some hazard.
But my frantic, full-beamed Mayday signal
only threw light on a de-iced porthole.

Inside that, another empty circle:
the fur-lined hood of your snorkel parka;
blank, faceless, blindly staring; driving on
regardless in the other direction.

Finding Your Own Feet

Like decades back, when dating got done
on the front porch, not across the seats

of a Chevy Duster, and for those making eyes
on the chaise longue the pool table rule applied:

one or both feet to remain on the carpet.
Like ratings: from A for Smooth

through C for Pass in a crowd, to E
for Spook, and although the spooks on campus

dismiss it as a sick, sick joke
they go weeping to the commissary, dateless

and heartbroken. Like economics when a coke
costs double if you're going steady,

or the freshman who blew five hundred
in the first term on female company,

or the redhead in detention who could prop
a cherry lipstick in her forced cleavage

then lower her mouth gingerly onto it,
or him that thought more than a handful

was wasted. Like the girls getting younger:
supple like rubber bands they talk braces

and bikini lines, wax off imaginary hairs
and touch their painted toes like gymnasts,

perfect to the nth degree of difficulty.
Like the history of American cycle riding

or the glittering career of a champion racer.
Like knowing Dempsey would have given

his right arm to be as hot in the saddle
as he was in the ring, and why not,

in the thin air round Salt Lake Velodrome
when the front man takes the line, and lifts

both arms and comes off the camber
like a beach bum down a Surf City breaker.

Shaved legs in the rain: beautiful like dolphin skin.
Like '68; the Tet offensive, senator Kennedy

but more to the point the Chicago Convention.
Like protest but more like pantomime.

Like Marxism; Groucho Marxism, when the Yippies
dump acid in the water supply, or conga

through the riot shields as if their conga
equalled one millipede showing off its new shoes

or a slow train kicking out its wheels
every fourth sleeper. Like asking

'how do you know you're on the side
of morality – you just do,' or showing

a clean pair of heels, or saying 'that's
an outrageous statement but I can explain it.'

Ivory

No more mularkey,
no baloney. No more cuffuffle
or shenanigans;

all that caboodle
is niet dobra. It will end
this minute.

No more fuss
or palaver; no more mush
or blarney. No flowers,

by request; no offence meant,
and none taken. No more blab,
none of that ragtag

and bobtail business,
or ballyhoo
or balderdash

and no jackassery, or flannel,
or galumphing.
Listen:

from this point forward
it's ninety-nine
and forty-four hundredths

per cent pure.
And no remarks
from the peanut gallery.

Not the Bermuda Triangle

but the melt down of a cast-iron relationship
or the downward spiral of a thirties biplane
onto the paddock where the torches are flaring;
a good time despite the head wind.

Of course there is a third party, but
our chap being a decent sort
will do the decent thing: that is
bluff it in a Brighton hotel

with two paid snoops outside the door
and a woman of experience in the adjoining room.
Later, at the club, he will get tight on good brandy
and as for the estate it is simply hard cheese.

Breakfast in bed, and on the tray
two halves of a hollowed grapefruit
like the ample cups of...
or coconut hooves to anticipate

the riding accident: the ditch, the service bus
with its full compliment of witnesses, the back-
firing Brough Superior and the uncontrollable mare...
Someone will have to tell her.

Someone will have to crash the party
where Madame ZaZa is tracing a pencil
along the life lines of their delicate feet.
Someone will have to steer her

out into the street, in and out
of the waiting landau and up to the charming flat
with its lashings and lashings of piping hot water
and the very last word in American plumbing.

Remembering the East Coast

First it was the oil tankers
spokeshaving their ironic rainbows
over the Channel.
Then that silly season
when the oil rigs blew

like bottles in a crate
of excited stout. In time
they were topped.
The seals took it badly, belly up
in the mouth of The Wash

but the Chunnel
was the final straw, its fracture
blowing bubble after bubble
of imported waste which they promised
would not matter.

Multiconglomerates! I was
a small tooth
in a grinding of cogs, a soft touch
reassigned from Birdstrike Prevention
to Torpedo Tracking. I'd done well.
Too well some said.

Naturally, my section
was ozone friendly, but frankly
we were scratching the tip of the iceberg.
Like organic farming:
it was small potatoes. Like my poster

on the canteen wall
which earned me the status
of a fifth columnist: our planet
from space, silver like a shilling
and its caustic legend: DON'T SPEND IT. SAVE IT.

At conference
how they roared at the chairman's address,
his much told fable
of the bald patents clerk
who resigned his post circa 1850

explaining 'Everything we need
is now invented.'
But alone I am with him; dipping the quill,
crossing the t of his signature,
blotting the i's

of his oddball opinion.

Working for the Mussel Farmers

The loving couple
    the townsfolk have christened them
for the way they link arms
    when they pick up provisions.
They are childless,
    but since their small ad
in the post office window
    I have been their boy:
shivering on the jetty
    in outsize waders,
waiting for their launch
    to muddy the shallows
then we rickrack
    back to their private inlet,
the skirt-length of the loch
    intact, unbroken
till we run out our seam
    of pierced white water.

It was late spring
    when they showed me the ropes:
how the lines are seeded,
    how the buoys are weighted.
Now, in the long evenings
    they roll cigarettes, sit
cross-legged on the landing stage
    before taking
to their floating fibreglass office
    to check on the forecast
or update the ledger.
    Then they appear
with the sun behind them:
    two upright shadows
in that translucent cabin
    like two hands washing
in a see-through basin;
    the palms of their stomachs
smoothing together,
    the fingers of their limbs

interlocking, engaging,
    and on still nights the ripples
of their unsuppressed movements
    fill the bay with a broadcast
of concentric signals.

    'Tyro' they shout for me,
or 'Tenderfoot', thinking me
    a little wet behind the ears.
In a cauldron
    over the evening's campfire
the tight lips are coaxed open.
    I part and sample their famous shellfish,
strange in flavour,
    perfect in appearance.

Zoom!

It begins as a house, an end terrace
in this case
   but it will not stop there. Soon it is
an avenue
   which cambers arrogantly past the Mechanics' Institute,
turns left
   at the main road without even looking
and quickly it is
   a town with all four major clearing banks,
a daily paper
   and a football team pushing for promotion.

On it goes, oblivious of the Planning Acts,
the green belts,
   and before we know it it is out of our hands:
city, nation,
   hemisphere, universe, hammering out in all directions
until suddenly,
   mercifully, it is drawn aside through the eye
of a black hole
   and bulleted into a neighbouring galaxy, emerging
smaller and smoother
   than a billiard ball but weighing more than Saturn.

People stop me in the street, badger me
in the check-out queue
   and ask 'What is this, this that is so small
and so very smooth
   but whose mass is greater than the ringed planet?'
It's just words
   I assure them. But they will not have it.